Twister greeting cards

Betsy Lurvink

FORTE PUBLISHERS

Contents

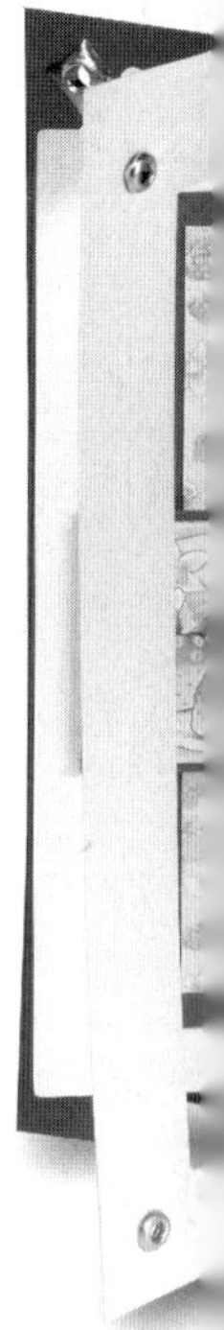

Original title: *Twisterkaarten*

ISBN 90 5877 451 1

This is a publication from
Forte Publishers BV
P.O. Box 1394
3500 BJ Utrecht
The Netherlands

For more information about the creative books available from Forte Uitgevers:
www.forteuitgevers.nl

Final editing: Gina Kors-Lambers, Steenwijk, the Netherlands
Photography and digital image editing: Fotografie Gerhard Witteveen, Apeldoorn, the Netherlands
Cover and inner design: BADE creatieve communicatie, Baarn, the Netherlands
Translation: Michael Ford, TextCase, Hilversum, the Netherlands

Preface

Twister cards are cards which consist of three different parts which you can decorate separately with eyelets, decorative stickers, border punches and Funny Fibres. When you have finished decorating them, you slide the three parts back together. Once you have put it back together, you can twist the card to display a different scene. You can see the main scene on the front, whilst the back of the inner twister card often has a surprise.

The cards are available as a rectangle, octagon, square, oval, circle and flower. There are four different coloured cards of the same type in a pack and the basic colours are always white and ivory. Combining white or ivory with a darker colour makes these cards look very colourful.

Make a twister card and give it your own twist.

Betsy

Thanks:
John Weezepoel (www.allergaartje.nl) who gave me the idea for these cards, my son Thijs who thought of the name **Twister** card, Marianne Design and Marij Rahder for providing the cutting sheets and my husband Gerard for all the typing he did.

Techniques

Twister cards are available in six different shapes: rectangle, square, octagon, oval, circle and flower. The cards are available in packs of four different colours. Every pack contains a white card, an ivory card and two cards of a darker colour (red, blue, green or aubergine). The colours in the packs are different for each shape.

The twister cards consist of three separate parts which you can put back together. Remove the cards from the packaging and take the parts apart (cut them carefully with a knife). Combine a light colour with a dark colour (see photograph 1). Place the three separate parts on the table: the inner part is the twister card, the part with the two feet is the inner border and the largest part is the outer border. The opening in the inner border can be used as a template of the twister card which you can use to cut a shape out of the paper of your choice and then stick to the twister card. Always start decorating the front and back of the twister card. If you wish, make the pictures 3D (see photograph 2). The light coloured inner and outer borders are good to use for embossing. Punch eyelets in the corners, 0.8 cm from the edge. Punch eyelets in the dark coloured inner and outer borders. Decorate the borders with border stickers, Funny Fibres and small pictures from cutting sheets (see photograph 3). Put the card back together once you have decorated all the parts by first carefully placing the inner border in the outer border and then placing the twister card in the middle (see photograph 4).

Embossing

Place the stencil on the part of the card that you wish to emboss and stick them together using non-permanent adhesive tape. Turn the stencil and the card over and place them on a light box. Carefully push the pattern into the card using an embossing stylus. Repeat this, if necessary. Finally, remove the stencil from the card.

Eyelets

Small, coloured eyelets can be punched into the card using a suitable toolkit. There are 10 different metallic colours in different shapes: flower, star, circle, triangle, square, heart and mini-circles. There 72 eyelets in a box. Fun eyelets are used for these cards for the following:

1. To decorate a border or a twister card.
2. To thread a pretty coloured tread or ribbon through a card for decoration.
3. To hang a card, a label or a part of a pattern on a card.

1. *Separate the different parts of the card. Keep the small square in a safe place.*

2. *Decorate the front and back of the twister card.*

3. *Decorate the inner and outer borders by embossing, using eyelets and adding border stickers.*

4. *Put the different parts of the card back together.*

Punching eyelets

Punch a hole in the place where you wish to have an eyelet. Use the hollow pipe from the toolkit and a (200 gram) hammer. Press the eyelet through the hole, turn the card over and hit the eyelet using the striking tool from the toolkit and a hammer to hammer the back of the eyelet in place. Use an eyelet mat as a surface to work on. This mat is ideal for indicating the position of an eyelet.

Bradletz

These are mini split pins in gold and silver which are ideal for attaching labels to a card.

Making 3D pictures

Most cutting sheets are designed so that the parts which you need to make 3D pictures have been drawn in steps (step sheets). Use photo glue to stick the first layer on the card. Cut the other parts out, puff them up slightly, stick pieces of foam tape behind them and stick them in the correct place. Sometimes, you don't use all the pictures because fewer layers are used. If you do not use all the pictures, you can then use them on the inner or outer borders of the card.

Separating sheets

This is 130 gram paper which is available in the same colour as the cards which is ideal to use as a background or when using layers (a protruding border).

Materials

- ❑ *Twister cards: square, rectangle, octagon, oval, circle and flower*
- ❑ *Cutting sheets: Marij Rahder (MR), Marianne Design (MD) and Marjoleine (M)*
- ❑ *Pattern paper (Marjoleine)*
- ❑ *Separating sheets*
- ❑ *Decorative frames*
- ❑ *Fun eyelets*
- ❑ *Round Bradletz*
- ❑ *Embellishments*
- ❑ *Charms*
- ❑ *Funny Fibres*
- ❑ *Border stickers*
- ❑ *Cutting mat, knife and ruler*
- ❑ *3D scissors*
- ❑ *Foam tape and photo glue*

Cards in the preface

What you need:

- ❑ *Twister cards: circle and rectangle (red/white)*
- ❑ *Cutting sheets: K2322 and V2433 (MR)*
- ❑ *Fun eyelets (gold)*
- ❑ *Round Bradletz (silver)*
- ❑ *Deco embossing templates (DE03 and DE04)*
- ❑ *Text Charms*
- ❑ *Separating sheets: red and white*

Card on page 1

Cut a circle (Ø 8.5 cm) out of the background paper. Prick two holes in it and use Bradletz to secure the "Special for you" Charms to it. Stick the gnome on it. Stick the circle on the red twister card and stick the circular picture of the gnome with cherries on the back.

Inner border: Emboss flowers and leaves in the corners and punch four eyelets.
Outer border: Punch four eyelets and add some strawberries and cherries.

Card on page 3

Cut a rectangle (10.5 x 5 cm) out of the red separating sheet and a rectangle (9.5 x 4 cm) out of the background paper. Stick these rectangles on the white twister card. Stick the squares with fruit on the red separating sheet and cut them out leaving a border. Stick the (oval) scene with the gnome on the back with some strawberries.
Inner border: Punch eyelets in the corners and add a white border sticker.
Outer border: Emboss the border and attach an eyelet in the corners.

Flowers

Who shall I give this pretty basket of flowers to?

What you need:

- ❑ *Twister cards: circle (green/ivory) and oval (aubergine/ivory)*
- ❑ *Cutting sheets: flower basket (MR), tulips and sunflowers (MD)*
- ❑ *Separating sheets: ivory and green*
- ❑ *K & Company scrapbook paper (Dorset 0916)*
- ❑ *Deco embossing template (DE03)*
- ❑ *Ivory eyelets*
- ❑ *Fun eyelets (green)*
- ❑ *Round Bradletz (silver)*
- ❑ *Border ornament punch (sunflower)*
- ❑ *Pattern paper: nos. 8 and 11*
- ❑ *Gold border sticker*
- ❑ *Mini-envelopes template*

Card 1

Front: Cut a circle (Ø 8.2 cm) out of a green separating sheet and another circle (Ø 8 cm) out of the background paper. Stick these circles on the ivory twister card. Stick the basket of flowers on the circles.
Back: Cut a circle (Ø 8.4 cm) out of the background paper and another circle (Ø 4.2 cm) out of green paper and stick them together. Punch three eyelets and stick the flowers on the circle. Stick everything on the back.

Inner border
Punch the two sides. Use foam tape to stick small flowers in the corners.
Outer border
Emboss some branches and leaves in the four corners. Punch two eyelets.

Card 2

Follow the description given for card 1, except cut a circle (Ø 7.5 cm) out of pattern paper for the front and another circle (Ø 9 cm) for the back.

Card 3

Copy the oval twice onto pattern paper no. 8. Cut them out and stick them on the

1.
2.
3.
4.

aubergine twister card. Stick the bunch of tulips on it.

Back: Use the template to cut an envelope out of pattern paper no. 8 and use Bradletz to attach it to the card. Allow a couple of tulips to protrude.

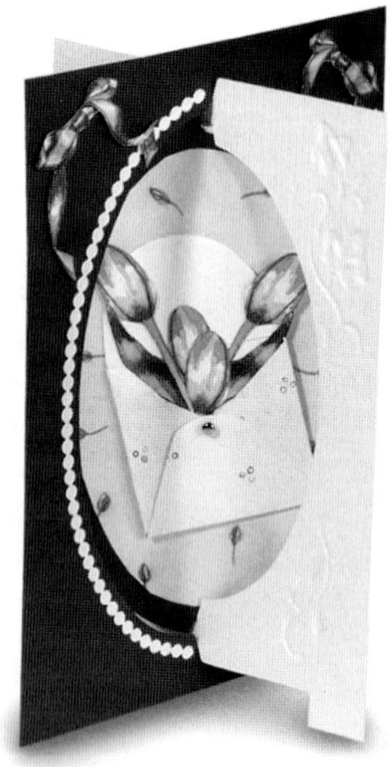

Back of card 3

Inner border

Emboss a number of branches.

Outer border

Stick the tulips on the front and stick a white border sticker on the back.

Card 4

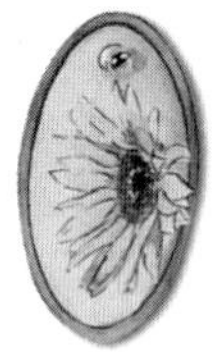

Copy the oval twice onto pattern paper no. 11. Cut them out and stick them on the front and back of the twister card. Cut out the envelope. Use a Bradletz to attach the sunflower label to it and stick it on the card. Allow a couple of sunflowers to protrude.

Back: Stick the bunch of sunflowers on the back with a ribbon.

Inner border

Stick a basket of flowers Charms in the corners with a ribbon and add a border sticker.

Outer border

Emboss a couple of leaves and branches.

The beach

What is nicer than a day at the beach?

What you need:

- *Twister cards: rectangle and square (blue/white)*
- *Cutting sheets: V2430 and K2320 (MR)*
- *Pattern paper no. 10*
- *Separating sheets: dark blue and light blue*
- *Fun eyelets (dark blue)*
- *Deco embossing template (DE01)*
- *Square frame embossing stencil*
- *Charms: Holiday (Make Me)*
- *Blue decorative frames*
- *White border sticker*
- *Transparent square stickers*

Card 1

Emboss a square on the white twister card. Stick the square with the seagull on it. Cut a square (9 x 9 cm) out of the pattern paper and stick it on the back. Cut out the four squares with seagulls and stick them on a blue separating sheet. Stick a transparent sticker on each square. Cut them out and stick them on the card.

Inner border

Punch a square eyelet in the corners and add border stickers.

Outer border

Emboss the border and punch an eyelet in the corners.

Card 2

Cut a square (9 x 9 cm) out of the pattern paper. Stick the beach scene on it and stick it on the dark blue twister card. Cut a square (8 x 8 cm) out of the pattern paper and stick it on the back. Cut out the squares with the people on the beach and stick them on a dark blue separating sheet. Cut them out leaving a border and stick them on the card. Cut out the beach tents and stick them on the card.

Inner border

Emboss the border and punch an eyelet in the corners.

Outer border

Punch a flower eyelet in the four corners. Stick white border stickers on the front and back.

Card 3

Round off the corners of the twister card. Stick the smallest decorative frames on the background sheet, cut them out and stick them on the front and the back of the twister card. Stick a couple of seagulls on one side and two squares with seagulls on the other. Stick the squares first on a blue separating sheet and then cut them out leaving a border.

Back of card 3

Inner border

Punch six eyelets and add white border stickers.

Outer border

Punch the border. Add the large decorative frame and punch an eyelet in the corners.

Card 4

Cut a rectangle (10.5 x 6.5 cm) out of pattern paper. Stick this on a light blue separating sheet, cut it out leaving a border and stick it on the twister card. Stick the kite scene on it. Use foam tape to stick the kite on the picture and then add a black thread. Emboss the parasol Charms in two corners on the back. Stick the deck chairs on two different shades of blue paper, cut them out leaving a border and stick them on the card. Stick the parasol near the ladies in the grass.

Inner border

Emboss the border and stick a decorative frame on the back.

Outer border

Punch a heart eyelet in the four corners and add a border sticker.

1.
2.
3.
4.

A boy

A traditional blue boy's card.

What you need:

- ❑ *Twister cards: rectangle and square (blue/ivory)*
- ❑ *Baby cutting sheets: V2436 (MR), AK 1008, KL 3003 and MD 1005*
- ❑ *Fun eyelets (light blue and gold)*
- ❑ *Round Bradletz (gold)*
- ❑ *Deco embossing template (DE02)*
- ❑ *Pattern paper no. 11*
- ❑ *Separating sheets: white and dark blue*
- ❑ *Light blue decorative frame*
- ❑ *Embellishment: ABC blue*
- ❑ *Funny Fibres (blue)*
- ❑ *Charms: Baby (Make Me) and EE 4302*
- ❑ *Embellishment: baby*

Card 1

Stick part of the background sheet behind the window of the light blue decorative frame and cut it out. Stick it on a dark blue separating sheet (10.5 x 7 cm) and stick it on the twister card. Stick the baby and the cuddly toy on it.

Back of card 1

Back: Cut out two squares (baby rusk and baby bottle) and stick them on dark blue squares (5 x 5 cm). Punch a light blue eyelet in the corners. Stick everything on the card.

Inner border
Stick the light blue frame on the front and a strip and a couple of small patterns on the back.
Outer border
Emboss the entire border.

Card 2

Cut a rectangle out of the background paper (6 x 4 cm) and out of the ivory paper (8 x 7 cm). Stick them together and attach the heart using a Bradletz. Stick this on the twister card. Stick the baby with the rusk on it.
Back: Cut squares out of ivory paper (7 x 7 cm), dark blue paper (6 x 6 cm) and background paper (5.5 x 5.5 cm). Stick them together and stick the square with the rattle in the middle. Punch a blue eyelet in the corners.
Inner border
Emboss the border with baby patterns.
Outer border
Punch a star eyelet in the four corners and add a couple of small patterns.

Card 3

Cut two squares (8 x 8 cm) out of the pattern paper and one square (8.5 x 8.5 cm) out of a blue separating sheet. Stick them together and stick them on the front and back of the twister card.

Punch holes and use Bradletz to attach the letters "BABY".
Add the baby in the basket.
Stick the Embellishments and a couple of small pictures on the back.
Inner border
Punch four eyelets in the inner border and thread a Funny Fibre through them.
Outer border
Emboss the entire border.

Card 4

Cut two rectangles (10.4 x 6 cm) out of pattern paper and stick them on an ivory separating sheet. Cut them out leaving a small border. Add a cradle and a bear with a flower to the front and the word "BABY" with ducks and a ribbon to the back.
Inner border
Emboss the border with hearts and a rattle.
Outer border
Punch six blue eyelets and thread a Funny Fibre through them.

1.
2.
3.
4.

1.
2.
3.
4.

A girl

A girl's card in aubergine and lilac.

What you need:
- ❑ *Twister cards: octagon and flower (aubergine/ivory)*
- ❑ *Baby cutting sheets: V2435 (MR) and AK 1008 MB (MD)*
- ❑ *Fun eyelets (lilac)*
- ❑ *Round Bradletz (gold)*
- ❑ *Deco embossing template (DE02)*
- ❑ *Pattern paper: nos. 7 and 8*
- ❑ *Separating sheets: aubergine and lilac*
- ❑ *Decorative frame: octagon (lilac)*
- ❑ *Charms: Baby (Make Me)*
- ❑ *Embellishment: baby*

Card 1

Stick the lilac frame on the twister card and stick the baby in the bath and the rattle on it. Stick a frame on pattern paper no. 7, cut it out and stick it on the back.

Cut the rusk, the bottle with the baby shoes and the text "BABY GIRL" out of the background paper and use foam tape to stick them on the card.

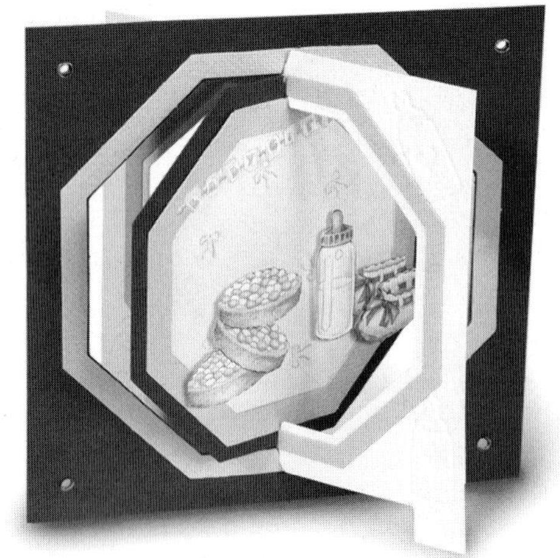

Back of card 1

Inner border
Stick the frame edges on the card and emboss baby bottles (Charms) in the corners.
Outer border
Stick the largest frames on the card and punch a lilac heart eyelet in the four corners.

Card 2

Copy the small flower shape onto the background paper and cut it out. Stick it on the twister card and stick the baby on it.
Back: Copy the flower shape onto a lilac separating sheet, cut it out and stick it on an aubergine separating sheet. Cut the flower out leaving a border. Use a Bradletz to attach the baby's head (Charms). Stick a couple of small pictures on the card.

Inner border

Punch a star eyelet in the four corners and add a couple of small pictures from the cutting sheet.

Outer border

Emboss the socks and the rattle.

Card 3

Cut two small flowers out of pattern paper no. 8 and stick them on the front and back of the twister card. Stick the bear on the front and the baby socks on the back.

Inner border

Emboss baby socks and punch eyelets in the corners.

Outer border

Punch a flower eyelet in the four corners and stick ducks and baby socks on the card.

Card 4

Copy two small octagon shapes onto an aubergine separating sheet, cut them out and stick them on both sides of the twister card. Stick the flowers on the front with a ribbon and the ABC Embellishments. For the back, cut out "HELLO BABY", stick it on pattern paper no. 8 and cut it out carefully. Emboss a cradle (Charms) in the middle of this and stick it on the card.

Inner border

Punch a star eyelet in the four corners and add a couple of small pictures.

Outer border

Emboss two rattles and two bottles and attach an eyelet in the four corners.

Summer

A summer card is always welcome.

What you need:
- ❑ *Twister cards: octagon (aubergine/ivory) and square (blue/ivory)*
- ❑ *Cutting sheets: roses (MR) and hydrangeas (MD)*
- ❑ *Frame sheets: octagon and square (lilac)*
- ❑ *Separating sheets: dark blue, lilac and aubergine*
- ❑ *Deco embossing template (DE03)*
- ❑ *Square frame embossing stencil*
- ❑ *Fun eyelets (pink and lilac)*
- ❑ *White border stickers*

Card 1

Stick a lilac frame on the background paper. Cut it out, stick it on the twister card and stick the rose on it.
Back: Copy the small octagon shape onto a lilac separating sheet. Cut it out and emboss a rose border on it. Stick two roses on it.
Inner border
Stick a lilac frame on the card. Punch a pink flower eyelet in the corners and stick small roses on the back.
Outer border
Emboss a petal in the four corners.

Card 2

Copy the small octagon onto a lilac separating sheet. Cut it out and emboss four branches on it. Stick it on aubergine paper and cut it out

Back of card 2

HOR-
TEN-
SIA
1.
2.
3.
4.

leaving a border. Stick the rose on it and stick this on the twister card.
Back: Stick a frame on aubergine paper.
Cut it out and stick it on the back of the twister card. Stick a couple of roses on it.

Inner border

Emboss the entire border.

Outer border

Punch a pink flower eyelet in each corner.
On the back, stick a rose in each corner.

Card 3

Stick the lilac frame on a lilac separating sheet and cut it out. Cut four squares out of the cutting sheet. Stick them on blue paper and cut them out leaving a border. Use foam tape to stick them on the card.
Back: Cut a square (8.5 x 8.5 cm) out of lilac paper and emboss a frame on it.
Stick a hydrangea on it.

Inner border

Emboss the inner border and punch a lilac eyelet in the corners.

Outer border

Punch a flower eyelet in the corners. Stick a border sticker on the front and back and add a couple of flowers.

Card 4

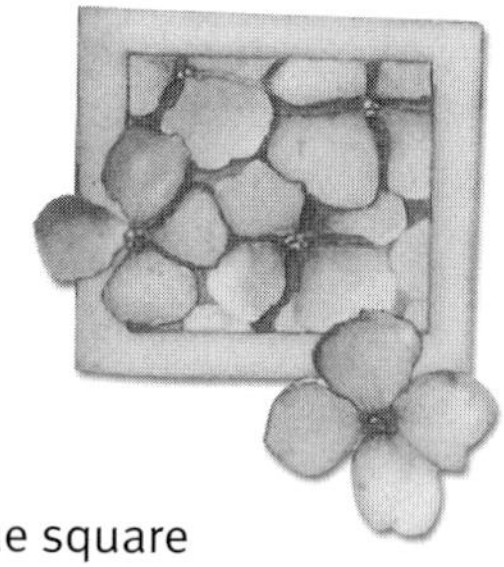

Cut a square (8 x 8 cm) out of a blue separating sheet and a square (7 x 7 cm) out of a lilac separating sheet. Emboss a square on the lilac square, stick it on the blue square and stick this on the twister card.
Use foam tape to stick the square hydrangea picture on the card.
Back: Cut a square (9 x 9 cm) out of blue paper and a square (8 x 8 cm) out of lilac paper. Stick the blue hydrangea on it.

Inner border

Punch a lilac flower eyelet in the corners and add white border stickers.

Outer border

Emboss the entire border.

Autumn

Attractive autumn cards are always elegant.

What you need:

- ❏ *Twister cards: rectangle and flower (red/white)*
- ❏ *Cutting sheets: Autumn and rose hip (MD)*
- ❏ *Separating sheet: white*
- ❏ *Deco embossing templates: DE01, DE03 and DE04*
- ❏ *Fun eyelets (gold)*
- ❏ *Pattern paper: nos. 8 and 12*
- ❏ *Gold sticker letters*
- ❏ *White border stickers*

Card 1

Copy the small flowers twice onto pattern paper no. 8. Cut them out and stick them on the front and back of the twister card. Stick the bunch of rose hips

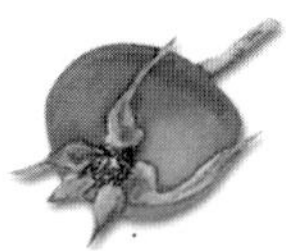

on the front and the tit with the rose hips on the back.

Inner border

Punch a star eyelet in the corners and add a couple of rose hips on both sides.

Outer border

Emboss a branch in the four corners.

Card 2

Copy the small flowers twice onto pattern paper no. 12. Cut them out and stick them on the front and back of the twister card. Stick the tit with berries on the card and stick the text "AUTUMN" and some berries on the other side.

Inner border

Emboss a wavy pattern in the four corners and punch a heart eyelet in the corners.

Outer border

Punch a heart eyelet in the four corners.

Card 3

Cut two rectangles (10.7 x 6 cm) out of pattern paper no. 8. Stick them on a white separating sheer and cut them out leaving a border. Stick them on the front and the back of the twister card and stick a twig of rose hips on them. Cut three squares out of the cutting sheet and stick them on the back.

Inner border
Emboss lines and dots on the border.
Outer border
Punch an eyelet in the corners and add border stickers.

Back of card 3

Card 4

Cut a rectangle (10.5 x 6 cm) out of the red separating sheet and another rectangle (11.5 x 7 cm) out of pattern paper no. 12. Stick them together and then stick them on the twister card. Stick the twig of berries and the text "AUTUMN" on them. Cut a rectangle (9.5 x 6 cm) out of the red separating sheet and another rectangle (8.5 x 5.5 cm) out of pattern paper no. 12. Stick them together and then stick them on the back of the twister card. Use foam tape to stick three squares on top.
Inner border
Punch an eyelet in the four corners.
Outer border
Emboss the entire border.

1.
2.
3.
4.
AUTUMN

Christmas in blue

A home-made

Christmas card

is always welcome.

What you need:

- ❑ *Twister cards: square and rectangle (blue/white)*
- ❑ *Separating sheets: white, light blue and dark blue*
- ❑ *Cutting sheets: Xmas (MD) and Christmas in blue (M)*
- ❑ *Pattern paper no. 5*
- ❑ *Star vellum*
- ❑ *Deco embossing template (DE05)*
- ❑ *Fun eyelets (blue)*
- ❑ *Round Bradletz (silver)*
- ❑ *Funny Fibres (blue)*
- ❑ *Mini-envelope template*
- ❑ *Square star art punch*
- ❑ *"Merry Christmas" computer text sheet*
- ❑ *Snowflakes decorative sticker*

Card 1

Front: Cut out the squares with houses. Stick them on a light blue separating sheet and cut them out leaving a border. Stick them on dark blue paper and cut them out again leaving a border. Stick them on the card.

Back: Copy the small square onto the pattern paper and use four eyelets to attach it to the twister card. Cut an envelope out of the pattern paper. Use Bradletz to stick the pieces together and stick it on the card. Cut the text "MERRY CHRISTMAS" (see Christmas in red and green) in the shape of a label. Stick it on blue paper and cut it out leaving a border. Punch an eyelet in the tip and thread a Funny Fibre through it. Place the label in the envelope.

Inner border

Stick a couple of snowflake stickers on the border.

Outer border

Punch six eyelets and thread blue Funny Fibre through them.

Card 2

For the front of the twister card, cut out five small squares with houses. Stick them on a dark blue separating sheet and cut them out leaving a border. Punch four squares out of light blue paper using the art punch and cut them

out. Stick everything on the card.
For the back of the twister card, follow the instructions given for card 1.

Back of card 2

Card 3

Copy the small blue rectangle twice onto a white separating sheet. Cut out the rectangles and emboss them. Stick them on the front and the back of the twister card. Stick the rectangular picture on the front. Cut out two squares, stick them on blue paper and cut them out again leaving a border. Stick them on the back.

Inner border
Emboss the border and punch an eyelet in the corners.

Outer border
Punch an eyelet in the corners and stick a couple of snowflake stickers on the border.

Card 4

Stick a decorative frame on the vellum, cut it out and stick it on the white twister card. Stick the robin redbreast in the window on a white separating sheet. Cut it out and use an eyelet to attach it to the twister card as a label. Stick a blue frame on the back. Cut out the rectangular holly picture, stick it on blue paper and cut it out leaving a border. Stick it on the card with the text "XMAS".

Inner border
Punch an eyelet in the corners and stick a couple of snowflake stickers on the border.

Outer border
Emboss Christmas trees and punch an eyelet in the corners.

1.
2.
3.
4.

1.
2.
3.
4.

Christmas in red and green

We send more and more home-made Christmas cards.

What you need:

- ❑ *Twister cards: circle (red/white) and square (green/white)*
- ❑ *Cutting sheets: K2327 (MR), AK 1010 (MD) and KL3006 (MD)*
- ❑ *Separating sheets: red and white*
- ❑ *Pattern paper no. 6*
- ❑ *Blue star vellum*
- ❑ *Blue decorative frame*
- ❑ *Red frame sheet*
- ❑ *Fun eyelets (gold and silver)*
- ❑ *Round Bradletz (gold)*
- ❑ *Mini-envelope template*
- ❑ *Border ornament punch (holly)*
- ❑ *Deco embossing template (DE06)*
- ❑ *Charms: Christmas MD*
- ❑ *Christmas label: EL4203*
- ❑ *White border sticker*
- ❑ *Computer text sheet*

Card 1

Cut a circle (Ø 8 cm) out of a red separating sheet. Use the Christmas decoration label to emboss a Christmas decoration on a white separating sheet, cut it out and use a Funny Fibre to attach it to the red circle. Stick this on the white twister card and stick the Father Christmas on it. Cut an envelope out of the pattern paper. Stick this on the back and stick the standing Father Christmas on it.

Inner border

Punch a flower eyelet in the four corners and stick decorative stickers on the border.

Outer border

Emboss stars on the border.

Card 2

Use a computer to make a whole page of the text "Merry Christmas" in gold letters and print it on 130 gram white paper. Stick this text behind the cut out Christmas wreath and stick this on a circle (Ø 8 cm) which has been cut out of a white separating sheet. Stick everything on the red twister card.

Back: Cut out half of the wreath and stick it on a circle (Ø 8 cm). Use a Bradletz to attach a clock Charms to it.

Inner border
Emboss stars in the four corners and stick a round, red frame on the border.
Outer border
Punch the border. Stick berries in the corners.

Back of card 3

Card 3

Cut a square out of vellum which is slightly smaller than the twister card. Use non-permanent adhesive tape to stick it on the twister card and punch a star eyelet in the corners. Carefully remove the adhesive tape. Punch an eyelet in the middle at the top and hang the label of the robin redbreast from it. Stick the Christmas bunnies on the other side and stick a holographic sticker in the corners.
Inner border
Punch eyelets in the corners and stick border stickers around the border.
Outer border
Punch eyelets in the corners and decorate the border with holographic stickers.

Card 4

Make this card according to the instructions given for card 3.
Snow: Tear two wavy lines out of a white separating sheet and stick the scene with the sledge on it.

Finally

Finally, a few tips:

- *Personalize your card by adding a wish or a poem.*
- *Stick or write your wish on the narrow inner border or the outer border of the card.*
- *Write the poem on a label and use a ribbon to tie it to the card.*
- *Place your wish or your poem in an envelope you have made yourself.*
- *Make templates for punching eyelets in the corners of the inner border and the outer border.*
- *For the square Twister cards:*
    - *Cut out a square (12.5 x 12.5 cm). Measure 0.8 cm from the corners and punch a hole (outer border).*
    - *Cut out a square (11 x 11 cm). Measure 0.8 cm from the border and punch a hole (inner border).*
- *Also make a template for the rectangular Twister cards:*
    - *The dimensions are 15 x 10.5 cm (outer border) and 13.5 x 9 cm (inner border).*

Many thanks to Kars in Ochten, the Netherlands for supplying the materials.

The materials used can be ordered by shopkeepers from:
Kars & Co BV in Ochten, the Netherlands. Tel: +31 (0)344 642864 or www.kars.nl
Also see my website: www.betsylurvink.nl